I0409720

JORDAN: A KEY U.S. PARTNER

HEARING

BEFORE THE

SUBCOMMITTEE ON
THE MIDDLE EAST AND NORTH AFRICA

OF THE

COMMITTEE ON FOREIGN AFFAIRS
HOUSE OF REPRESENTATIVES

ONE HUNDRED FOURTEENTH CONGRESS

SECOND SESSION

FEBRUARY 11, 2016

Serial No. 114–157

Printed for the use of the Committee on Foreign Affairs

Available via the World Wide Web: http://www.foreignaffairs.house.gov/ or
http://www.gpo.gov/fdsys/

U.S. GOVERNMENT PUBLISHING OFFICE

98–604PDF   WASHINGTON : 2016

For sale by the Superintendent of Documents, U.S. Government Publishing Office
Internet: bookstore.gpo.gov   Phone: toll free (866) 512–1800; DC area (202) 512–1800
Fax: (202) 512–2104   Mail: Stop IDCC, Washington, DC 20402–0001

COMMITTEE ON FOREIGN AFFAIRS

EDWARD R. ROYCE, California, *Chairman*

CHRISTOPHER H. SMITH, New Jersey
ILEANA ROS-LEHTINEN, Florida
DANA ROHRABACHER, California
STEVE CHABOT, Ohio
JOE WILSON, South Carolina
MICHAEL T. McCAUL, Texas
TED POE, Texas
MATT SALMON, Arizona
DARRELL E. ISSA, California
TOM MARINO, Pennsylvania
JEFF DUNCAN, South Carolina
MO BROOKS, Alabama
PAUL COOK, California
RANDY K. WEBER SR., Texas
SCOTT PERRY, Pennsylvania
RON DeSANTIS, Florida
MARK MEADOWS, North Carolina
TED S. YOHO, Florida
CURT CLAWSON, Florida
SCOTT DesJARLAIS, Tennessee
REID J. RIBBLE, Wisconsin
DAVID A. TROTT, Michigan
LEE M. ZELDIN, New York
DANIEL DONOVAN, New York

ELIOT L. ENGEL, New York
BRAD SHERMAN, California
GREGORY W. MEEKS, New York
ALBIO SIRES, New Jersey
GERALD E. CONNOLLY, Virginia
THEODORE E. DEUTCH, Florida
BRIAN HIGGINS, New York
KAREN BASS, California
WILLIAM KEATING, Massachusetts
DAVID CICILLINE, Rhode Island
ALAN GRAYSON, Florida
AMI BERA, California
ALAN S. LOWENTHAL, California
GRACE MENG, New York
LOIS FRANKEL, Florida
TULSI GABBARD, Hawaii
JOAQUIN CASTRO, Texas
ROBIN L. KELLY, Illinois
BRENDAN F. BOYLE, Pennsylvania

AMY PORTER, *Chief of Staff* THOMAS SHEEHY, *Staff Director*
JASON STEINBAUM, *Democratic Staff Director*

———

SUBCOMMITTEE ON THE MIDDLE EAST AND NORTH AFRICA

ILEANA ROS-LEHTINEN, Florida, *Chairman*

STEVE CHABOT, Ohio
JOE WILSON, South Carolina
DARRELL E. ISSA, California
RANDY K. WEBER SR., Texas
RON DeSANTIS, Florida
MARK MEADOWS, North Carolina
TED S. YOHO, Florida
CURT CLAWSON, Florida
DAVID A. TROTT, Michigan
LEE M. ZELDIN, New York

THEODORE E. DEUTCH, Florida
GERALD E. CONNOLLY, Virginia
BRIAN HIGGINS, New York
DAVID CICILLINE, Rhode Island
ALAN GRAYSON, Florida
GRACE MENG, New York
LOIS FRANKEL, Florida
BRENDAN F. BOYLE, Pennsylvania

CONTENTS

JORDAN: A KEY U.S. PARTNER

THURSDAY, FEBRUARY 11, 2016

HOUSE OF REPRESENTATIVES,
SUBCOMMITTEE ON THE MIDDLE EAST AND NORTH AFRICA,
COMMITTEE ON FOREIGN AFFAIRS,
Washington, DC.

The committee met, pursuant to notice, at 2 o'clock p.m., in room 2172 Rayburn House Office Building, Hon. Ileana Ros-Lehtinen (chairman of the subcommittee) presiding.

Ms. ROS-LEHTINEN. Thank you so much. The subcommittee will come to order. I know that our panelists are going to be stepping out here in a second.

We will have votes starting at possibly 3 o'clock or 3:15 so we will try to wrap up before then. After recognizing myself and Ranking Member Deutch for 5 minutes each for our opening statements, I will then recognize other members seeking recognition for 1 minute.

We will then hear from our witnesses, and without objection the prepared statements of our witnesses will be made a part of the record and members may have 5 days to insert statements and questions for the record subject to the length limitation in the rules.

The chair now recognizes herself for 5 minutes. In recent years, the Hashemite Kingdom of Jordan has turned into one of America's most important allies.

The King of Jordan had proven to be a reliable partner and someone who is committed to protecting our shared security interest.

With all of the violence, all of the turmoil in the region and the accompanying instability and insecurity, the U.S. has made a substantial commitment to strengthening our bilateral relations with the Kingdom.

That commitment was reflected in a renewal of our memorandum of understanding, MOU, with Jordan, which was signed a year ago last week.

This new MOU recognizes the importance of Jordan in the fight on the front lines against ISIS and radical fundamentalism as well as the Kingdom's leadership in taking in over 1 million refugees from Syria and Iraq.

Jordan's resources are already scarce and with the addition of over 1 million Syrian and Iraqi refugees, these resources are being strained to the limit—stretched to the limit.

That is why it is vital that we help Jordan shore up some of these resources, especially when it comes to the Kingdom's water needs and energy needs.

Through our MCC-Jordan Compact, a $275 million compact that nears its completion, we have invested in public-private partnership wastewater projects that are now operational and serving over 1 million people, many of whom are refugees.

I had the pleasure of visiting the As-Samra Wastewater Plant in 2014 with Mr. Deutch and its importance cannot be overstated.

I am also pleased that a local south Florida firm, Hazen and Sawyer, was the engineering firm that managed the project, proof that these MCC compacts and projects can benefit both the U.S. economy and also the host nations.

There are other projects and it is important that we begin to bring them to fruition. One of these will not only be important to alleviate the water shortage in Jordan but it has the potential to also improve the cooperation and bilateral relations between Israel and Jordan—the Red to Dead Project.

Continued U.S. investment in this sort of infrastructure project has enormous upside and can really be a game changer and it is critical that Congress remains supportive of these efforts.

There is also the benefit—the potential for collaborative work between Israel and Jordan in other areas that can be mutually beneficial, especially when it comes to Jordan's energy needs.

Jordan signed an agreement with Israel to import natural gas and, again, as with the wastewater project, this agreement has economic benefits for the U.S. as well with U.S.-based Noble Energy discovering the natural gas field off the coast of Israel and now ready, willing and able to begin production to help meet the growing natural gas demand in Jordan and elsewhere.

And it will be important that we continue to support these efforts and others just like them because Israel and Jordan have shared concerns, shared interests and it would be mutually beneficial for the two to work closely together.

We must also continue to support the good work of USAID—the good work that they are doing to help Jordan in its economy but also the work it does to strengthen the country's democracy and governance as well as female empowerment programs.

The Jordanian Government's commitment to political reform over these past few years has been commendable and it is clear that our programs have had a good amount of success based on the interest and the support from the government and the Jordanian people, a testament to how this is—how this International Republican Institute—IRI—has been able to expand from working in just a handful of districts when its programs first started in Jordan to now over 30 and seeking to expand further in the coming years.

These programs have had successes. We need to build upon the support these programs have received and work with the Kingdom to help strengthen democracy and governance in Jordan and to strengthen civil society.

On security, Jordan's needs are also substantial because of the Kingdom—the Kingdom has been such a staunch ally in the coalition against ISIS, and the stability and security of Jordan are vital if we are ever going to see a secure and stable region.

That is why I am pleased that the bill I introduced with Congressman Deutch and as well as Congresswomen Granger and Lowey, the U.S.-Jordan Defense Cooperation Act, has passed Congress just last night and will now make its way to the President's desk.

The bill recognizes Jordan's precarious situation and the need for the U.S. to support the King's effort against ISIS.

That is why it will allow for expedited sales of certain weapons and ammunition and excess defense articles that the Kingdom needs to secure its borders, to protect its citizens and to assist the coalition in the fight against ISIS.

But as the King reminded us when he visited us last month, we cannot keep a myopic focus on the fight against ISIS and think that it is just in Iraq and in Syria.

ISIS is spreading, it is gaining support elsewhere and it has shown that it has the capability to strike the West as well.

The King warned us not to lose sight of the threat that ISIS poses in Africa where it can gain a lot of support and use a lot of territory for safe havens, and we, obviously, can't lose sight of the threat ISIS poses to us here in the homeland.

This is an obvious difficult task. But it would be much more difficult were it not for the leadership and the willingness of our ally Jordan to take on this challenge together.

I look forward to expanding and strengthening our relationship with the Kingdom of Jordan in the coming months and years and I thank the King for his steadfast commitment to the security and stability of the region, and we welcome Ambassador Bouran with us today.

Thank you so much. Mr. Deutch is recognized.

Mr. DEUTCH. Thank you, Madam Chairman.

Madam Chairman, you have been a true champion of the U.S.-Jordan relationship and I thank you for the opportunity to discuss the challenges facing our two countries in depth today.

Thanks to our witnesses for being here today and for the work that your agencies do to promote a stable and prosperous Jordan and to advance the U.S.-Jordan cooperation. I would especially like to thank Ambassador Feierstein for his many years of service and wish him well in his retirement.

And I would like to take a moment to recognize the Jordanian Ambassador, Ambassador Bouran, who does a fantastic job here in Washington and is a valued resource to many on this subcommittee.

I am also pleased that legislation introduced by the chairman and me, the U.S.-Jordan Defense Cooperation Act, has now passed the House and Senate and is on its way to the President's desk.

I thank our colleagues for supporting this bipartisan legislation that will ensure that Jordan has the tools that it needs to confront regional challenges.

Just over a year ago, the United States and Jordan cemented our partnership in a new memorandum of understanding that increased U.S. assistance to Jordan from $600 million to $1 billion annually.

This increase reflects our commitment to Jordan's stability and recognition of the tremendous strain placed upon Jordan since the start of this hearing crisis as well as Jordan's willingness to partner in the fight against ISIS.

The conflict in Syria has fundamentally altered Jordan and its effects will be felt for years to come. Jordan, already a home to hundreds of thousands of Iraqi refugees from previous conflicts, has taken in over 635,000 Syrian refugees and that number only reflects those refugees who are officially registered with the UNHCR.

Jordanian officials estimate this number is probably much higher than that. In fact, most Syrian refugees aren't currently living in the two U.N.-run camps and have instead assimilated into Jordanian towns.

While Jordanian host communities have welcomed Syrian refugees into their communities, the influx has, of course, placed a strain on Jordan's already scarce resources, particularly water and energy.

Many of our USAID programs have focused on increasing access to water while reducing waste. In fact, USAID programs have brought fresh water and sanitation services to more than one-third of Jordan's population. We look forward to hearing more about these efforts from Assistant Administrator Alexander.

Chairman Ros-Lehtinen and I had the opportunity to visit the As-Samra Wastewater Treatment Plant, the product of the MCC compact awarded to Jordan in 2010.

The expansion of this plant will increase access to water for 3 million Jordanians and, as the chairman mentioned, we are pleased to see a south Florida company involved in such an important project.

U.S. assistance has also focused on expanding access to education as well as infrastructure building and teacher training.

We often talk about the potential for an entire lost generation of Syrian children and our continued focus on building and rehabilitating schools is a critical component to ensure that refugee children are able to access education in host communities.

I applaud Secretary Kerry's recent announcement of $267 million in assistance for education in Jordan. We all appreciate the Government of Jordan's willingness to keep its borders open to refugees and I acknowledge the security challenges that this poses.

But as fighting in Syria's southern front increases, more and more refugees will be seeking safe passage to Jordan. I am extremely sensitive to Jordan's ability to adequately screen those trying to enter the country and it is my hope that those waiting at its borders, those who do not pose a threat to Jordan's stability, will be admitted as swiftly as possible.

As the U.S. seeks to expand the contribution to the members of the international coalition to counter ISIS, Jordan has continually met our call to action.

King Abdullah has often the need for Arab states to lead this fight against extremism and Jordanian planes have been flying missions since the formation of the coalition.

Let me again offer condolences—our condolences—to the people of Jordan for the horrific loss of a Jordanian pilot at the hands of ISIS just 1 year ago.

But if we want our partners to step up, we must ensure that they have what they need to both be active participants in the coalition and to defend their own borders.

That is why the legislation I referenced earlier passed by the chairman and me along with our Appropriations Committee colleagues Chairman Granger and Ranking Member Lowey is so critical.

Our bill will ensure the timely transfer of certain defense articles to the Kingdom. The King understands the importance of regional stability and recognizes the need to confront ISIS while working to find a political solution to the conflict in Syria and we appreciate the ability to consult regularly with him.

As we wait to see if talks can restart, I would just again note that as long as Assad is in power we will not be able to stem the flow of refugees from Syria or to defeat ISIS.

While the refugee crisis has no doubt strained Jordan's economy and resources, there are steps that can be taken now to reduce some of these pressures.

The lifting of various barriers to work for Syrian refugees will help refugees contribute to their communities. Economic investment will shore up jobs for Jordanians.

Cooperation with Israel on the Red to Dead project will help increase Jordan's access to water, and I thank the Kingdom for its commitment to peace with Israel and its recent efforts to reduce tensions at the Temple Mount.

The King can play a vital role in preserving the status quo as Israel has committed to do and I hope that any roadblocks in implementing the agreement brokered by Secretary Kerry to install cameras at the Temple Mount can soon be worked through.

In addition, I am alarmed by reports just this morning that certain members of Parliament are threatening to topple the government if Jordan moves ahead with the deal to import gas from Israel's Leviathan Field.

This deal has the potential to bring much needed energy sustainability to Jordan.

Madam Chairman, there is certainly a lot more to discuss when it comes to the depth of U.S. cooperation with Jordan and the increasingly important role that a stable Jordan plays in the region.

And I look forward to hearing more from our witnesses, and I yield back.

Ms. Ros-Lehtinen. Thank you so much, Mr. Deutch.

Mr. Cicilline is recognized.

Mr. Cicilline. Thank you, Madam Chair.

Thank you, Chairman Ros-Lehtinen and Ranking Member Deutch for calling this hearing on Jordan and our relationship and thank you to the witnesses.

I look forward to hearing from you about how our strong partnership with the Kingdom of Jordan can continue, particularly at this critical time in our shared fight against violent extremism as well as a pivotal moment in the resolution of the Israeli-Palestinian conflict.

I want to welcome Ambassador Bouran and again acknowledge her extraordinary leadership here in Washington and I would also like to express my appreciation to the Kingdom of Jordan for its leadership and its commitment to the coalition to defeat ISIL.

Jordan's actions s part of this coalition have been significant and difficult, notably, air strikes that have been conducted, Jordan's allowing foreign forces to use its bases, Jordan's sharing of intelligence with coalition partners, and we have a very long and close relationship with the Kingdom and look forward to continued and deepening cooperation.

The people and the Government of Jordan know all too well how ISIL's actions create instability and fear, which is why Jordan is hosting more than 630,000 refugees from Syria, and we appreciate this incredible sacrifice and remain committed to support Jordan's crisis management effort through increased economic support.

I had the opportunity to visit Jordan last March. As part of that visit I traveled to the Zaatari refugee camp and saw first hand the extraordinary challenges facing the Kingdom of Jordan and the extraordinary work being done.

And I look forward to the testimony of the witnesses today and working with the administration and my colleagues to further strengthen our important relationship with the Kingdom of Jordan.

And I yield back.

Ms. ROS-LEHTINEN. Thank you, Mr. Cicilline.

Ms. Frankel is recognized.

Ms. FRANKEL. Thank you, Madam Chair.

And I thank you for this opportunity because I have to leave for a markup in a few minutes—I mean, a vote at Transportation.

But I wanted to start. I thank you for the witnesses being here and I visited Jordan this year on a personal trip, and I just want to say for anyone who has never been there what a beautiful country it is, just magnificent—beautiful sites and beautiful people.

And I want to also thank—I see our Ambassador here—just thank you to the people of Jordan for opening their arms to the refugees.

I had an opportunity when I was there to meet with some women and children who had fled Syria and the issue that just kept coming up over and over that Mr. Deutch referenced to was their inability to do any work and to supplement the very pittance, really, of aid that they are getting.

So I would just be curious whether—I know there has been some discussions to maybe have some relief in that area. So I would be curious as to that.

I also would be interested to know what kind of work we are doing to enable Jordan to boost its economy. I was told that there is some work going on there.

And I would also be interested to know whether any of it involves trying to advertise or boost up its tourism because I will tell you, I have been all over the world and going—we went to the desert where "Lawrence of Arabia" was filmed. It was amazing. Well, there is a lot of historic sites there.

So I will be curious about the tourism industry. But on a more somber note, what is going on in Syria is so horrific and I am very interested in knowing what you—because the witnesses that are here—what you believe is the impact of Russia now intervening in Syria because I have heard that the rebel forces are being decimated and I know we have aid programs to the rebels and I am just wondering whether it is even worthwhile programs now.

And so I would like to get your insight on that. So when I leave I am not going to be rude. I have to go vote. But I am going to catch up and whatever you say somebody will take notes and tell me and I will try to come back.

Thank you very much for being here.

Ms. ROS-LEHTINEN. Thank you, Ms. Frankel.

We know that you are a professional all the time so there is no doubt when she says that she means it, and she has pointed out the benefits of private travel.

She got to visit where ''Lawrence of Arabia'' was. Mr. Deutch and I on congressional travel went to a wastewater plant. So that is quite a difference.

But now we are pleased to introduce our panelists. We welcome back Ambassador Gerald Feierstein, who is the principal deputy assistant secretary of the Bureau of Near Eastern Affairs.

Previously, the Ambassador served as our Ambassador to Yemen from 2010 to 2013 and has served in different postings throughout the Middle East, including as deputy chief of mission in Islamabad and deputy consul-general in Jerusalem. Thank you for your service and we look forward to your testimony, Mr. Ambassador.

Next, we welcome back Assistant Administrator Paige Alexander of the Bureau of the Middle East of USAID. Previously, Ms. Alexander has served as assistant administrator of the Bureau for Europe and Eurasia as well as associate director of Project Liberty at Harvard University's John F. Kennedy School of Government.

She has also served on the board of the Basic Education Coalition and the Project on the Middle East Democracy. Welcome back.

And last but certainly not least, we would like to welcome Fatema Sumar, who is the regional deputy vice president for—listen to these areas of the world—Europe, Asia, the Pacific and Latin America, wow—for the Millennium Challenge Cooperation's Department of Compact Operations.

Previously, Ms. Sumar was the deputy assistant secretary of state for South and Central Asian affairs and before that she was a congressional aide in the Senate Foreign Relations Committee, and I hear that Mr. Connolly used to be an aide in that—I have heard that before.

I thank you, Mr. Ambassador. We will begin with you.

STATEMENT OF THE HONORABLE GERALD M. FEIERSTEIN, PRINCIPAL DEPUTY ASSISTANT SECRETARY, BUREAU OF NEAR EASTERN AFFAIRS, U.S. DEPARTMENT OF STATE

Ambassador FEIERSTEIN. Thank you so much, Chairman Ros-Lehtinen, Ranking Member Deutch, distinguished members of the committee. Thank you for inviting me to discuss our relationship with the Hashemite Kingdom of Jordan today.

Let me also thank you for your continued support to Jordan over the years and in particular to express our thanks for your championing the United States-Jordan Defense Cooperation Act.

Now that this legislation has passed we look forward to expediting consideration of letters of offer to sell defense articles and services to the Kingdom of Jordan, thereby shrinking the delivery time for these articles even more.

As you note in the title to this hearing, Jordan is a key partner for the United States and has played a vital role in addressing virtually all of the highest priority challenges that the United States is facing in the Middle East.

From countering the threat of Daesh and supporting a peaceful political transition in Syria to expanding prosperity across the region, Jordan has been an essential ally.

The King is returning to Washington later this month and I know that President Obama looks forward to discussing many of these issues directly with him when they meet.

Nowhere is the strength of our relationship more apparent than our shared efforts against the threat of Daesh and other extremists.

Jordan is a committed leader in the global coalition to counter ISIL and the regional campaign against Daesh. Jordanian air force pilots regularly fly missions as part of Operation Inherent Resolve and have shown no sign of decreasing their tempo.

As part of our broader coalition efforts against Daesh, King Abdullah has called upon the international community to challenge Daesh's recruiting.

We are working hand in hand with our Jordanian counterparts to expose the false narrative of Daesh and other extremist groups and to deprive Daesh of financial resources.

Jordan has been a critical partner in international security efforts around the world for many years. In 1996, the United States designated Jordan as a major non-NATO ally. They are also a member of the Global Initiative to Combat Nuclear Terrorism.

Just last month during the King's visit, Secretary Kerry signed a joint action plan with Jordan to combat the smuggling of nuclear and radioactive materials, expressing our intent to work together to prevent, detect and respond to nuclear smuggling incidents.

Jordan has also been an integral part of the political process, spearheading efforts to reach a political transition in Syria through the International Syria Support Group.

Today, Foreign Minister Judeh joined Secretary Kerry in Munich during a meeting of this group as they deliberate on next steps to resolve the crisis in Syria.

We are also deeply appreciative of Jordan's crucial role in efforts to achieve a lasting peace between Israelis and Palestinians.

Jordan continues to demonstrate determination and resolve in support of our shared goals of reaching a two-state solution to the conflict and bringing an end to the vicious cycles of violence.

Since the signing of its peace treaty with Israel in 1994, Jordan's engagement on Israeli-Palestinian issues has been critical to our ongoing efforts to advance peace and stability in the region including this past fall when Jordan worked closely with us to help defuse tensions in Jerusalem on the Haram al-Sharif Temple Mount compound.

However, our partnership with Jordan goes beyond our two Governments. Trade between our two countries remain strong. Our free trade agreement with Jordan signed in 2000 was our first in the Arab world.

Total bilateral trade reached $2.8 billion in 2015 and you can now find a number of Jordanian goods in U.S. markets from cosmetics and jewelry to air conditioners and pharmaceuticals.

Jordanians, meanwhile, have access to Florida orange juice, Boeing airplanes and countless other U.S. products and services recognized for their quality.

As part of our commitment to Jordan's security and stability during this critical time, we are providing Jordan with robust security and economic assistance.

Last year, we signed a memorandum of understanding with Jordan signalling our intent to provide the Kingdom with $1 billion annually in security and economic assistance from Fiscal Year 2015 to Fiscal Year 2017 with Congress' generous support.

I know my colleague will further discuss our economic support but I wanted to note that Jordan received $385 million in Foreign Military Financing in Fiscal Year 2015, making it the third largest FMF recipient in the world. We will continue our robust support this year.

Before I conclude, I would like to address one issue that I know you are aware was an urgent topic of discussion during the King's recent visit.

Jordan currently hosts more than 635,000 registered Syrian refugees. We are working closely with the Jordanian Government on solutions to alleviate the strain on the country including how to handle ongoing humanitarian challenges for the 22,000 refugees on the Syrian-Jordanian border.

Chairman Ros-Lehtinen, Ranking Member Deutch, our partnership with Jordan remains strong and our military coordination and assistance has never been closer.

From their counter-Daesh activities to Jordan's active participation in a number of peacekeeping operations around the world, Jordan is a strong friend and an essential partner in our pursuit of regional peace and prosperity.

Thank you for the opportunity to testify. I look forward to taking your questions.

[The prepared statement of Ambassador Feierstein follows:]

Testimony
Before the House Foreign Affairs Committee
Subcommittee on the Middle East and North Africa
Jordan: A Key U.S. Partner
Statement of
Ambassador Gerald M. Feierstein,
Principle Deputy Assistant Secretary for Near Eastern Affairs

February 11, 2016

Chairman Ros-Lehtinen, Ranking Member Deutch, distinguished members of the Committee, thank you for inviting me to discuss our relationship with the Hashemite Kingdom of Jordan. Let me also thank you for all of your support to Jordan over the years, as well as the warm reception you gave King Abdullah during his visit last month.

As you note in the title to this hearing, Jordan is a key partner for the United States. Our relationship with Jordan is deep, spanning decades. Jordan plays a vital role in addressing virtually all the highest priority challenges the U.S. faces in the Middle East, from countering the threat of Da'esh and supporting a peaceful political transition in Syria, to expanding prosperity across the region. As Secretary Kerry said almost a year ago on February 20, 2015: "We simply could not find a country that has been more willing to be a good stand up, get-the-job-done partner than the Kingdom of Jordan." President Obama looks forward to discussing this cooperation with King Abdullah when he visits Washington later this month.

Nowhere is this relationship more apparent than in our shared efforts against the threat of Da'esh and other extremists. Jordan is a committed leader in the Global Coalition to Counter ISIL and the regional campaign against Da'esh. Royal Jordanian Air Force pilots regularly fly missions as part of Operation Inherent Resolve and, indeed, lost one of their own a year ago when Captain Al-Kasasbeh was burned alive in an especially horrific display of barbarity by Da'esh. Jordan remains committed to the air campaign in Syria and Iraq and has shown no sign of decreasing its tempo.

As part of our broader Coalition efforts against Da'esh, King Abdullah has called upon the international community -- and in particular the Muslim world -- to challenge Da'esh's recruiting. U.S. diplomats are working hand-in-hand with their Jordanian counterparts to expose the false lure of Da'esh and other extremist groups, organizing events, for example, that catalyze government and civil society cooperation to tackle the complex challenge of countering extremist propaganda, recruiting foreign terrorist fighters, and depriving Da'esh of financial resources.

Jordan has been a key partner in international security efforts around the world. In 1996, the United States designated Jordan as a major non-NATO ally. Jordan is also a member of the Global Initiative to Combat Nuclear Terrorism and the Proliferation Security Initiative. Last month, during King Abdullah's visit, Secretary Kerry signed a joint action plan with Jordan to combat the smuggling of nuclear and radioactive materials, expressing the intent of our governments to work together to prevent, detect, and respond to nuclear smuggling incidents. Jordan shares this administration's firm conviction that nuclear smuggling is a critical and ongoing global danger and it stands ready to join a coordinated, global response to contain that threat.

Another key area of cooperation between Jordan and the United States has been our efforts to seek a resolution to the war in Syria. Jordan has been an integral part of the political process spearheading efforts to reach a political transition in Syria through the International Syria Support Group. Indeed, Foreign Minister Judeh joined Secretary Kerry today in Munich during a meeting of this group as they deliberate on next steps to resolve the crisis in Syria and to address the immediate humanitarian needs of the Syrian people.

We are also deeply appreciative of Jordan's crucial role in international efforts to achieve a lasting peace between Israelis and Palestinians. Jordan continues to demonstrate determination and resolve in support of our shared goal of reaching a two-state solution to the conflict and bringing an end to the vicious cycles of violence. Since the signing of its peace treaty with Israel in 1994, Jordan's engagement on Israeli-Palestinian issues has been critical to our ongoing efforts to advance peace and stability in the region, including this past fall when Jordan worked closely with us to help defuse tensions in Jerusalem at the Haram al-Sharif/Temple Mount compound.

Our partnership with Jordan goes beyond our two governments. Trade between our two countries has never been stronger. Starting with the Qualifying Industrial Zones and now the Free Trade Agreement, total bilateral trade reached 3.5 billion in 2014. As a result of the FTA, which in 2000 was the very first signed in the Arab world, you can find Petra Engineering's air conditioning solutions, Hikma's pharmaceutical products, as well as Jordanian cosmetics, jewelry, and camping gear in U.S. markets. Jordanians, meanwhile, have access to apples from Washington state, Boeing airplanes and countless other U.S. products and services that are recognized for their quality and trustworthiness.

On a people-to-people level, the United States and Jordan are also working closely together. Approximately 7,300 Jordanians have participated in the State Department's various exchange programs. Our alumni include government ministers, journalists, artists, and educators. As part of the Fulbright program, for example, 30 Jordanians are currently studying or teaching in the United States, and 33 Americans are doing the same in Jordan.

Robust Assistance

As part of our commitment to Jordan's security and stability during this critical time, we are providing Jordan with robust security and economic assistance. Last year, we signed a Memorandum of Understanding with Jordan stating our intent to provide the Kingdom with $1 billion annually in security and economic assistance from FY 2015 to FY 2017, with Congress's generous support. Last fiscal year, as part of that MOU, $615 million went into our Economic Support Fund programs that directly help the Jordanian people through USAID programming, which I know my colleague will further discuss.

Jordan also received $385 million in Foreign Military Financing in FY 2015, making it the third-largest FMF recipient in the world, and we will continue our robust support this year. This security assistance helps Jordan secure its borders, participate in coalition activities, and build the core capacity of its armed forces. Additionally, Jordan has also been one of the largest recipients of counterterrorism assistance worldwide, receiving over $50 million since FY 2010 in Non-Proliferation, Anti-terrorism, Demining and Related Activities (NADR)/Anti-Terrorism Assistance (ATA) training for law enforcement officials.

Over the last year we have expedited several security systems to Jordan and improved our coordination with the Jordanian military to ensure our assistance matches Jordan's most urgent needs. Since the King's visit last February, the United States funded and notified the lease of eight UH-60A helicopters for Jordan, five of which have been delivered. These will be used by Jordan's Rapid Reaction Force, a crisis response element of the Border Guard Force. To better equip the Jordan Armed Forces, we have also delivered thousands of Night Vision Devices, millions of rounds of ammunition and thousands of small arms, and hundreds of aerial munitions. The U.S. has also completed a $93 million effort to expand the Jordan Border Security System that enables that country to monitor activity along the entirety of its borders with both the Syria and Iraq.

Refugees

Before I conclude, I would like to address one issue that was an urgent topic of discussion during King Abdullah's recent visit. According to the UN High Commissioner for Refugees, Jordan currently hosts more than 635,000 registered Syrian refugees. This rapid influx of refugees has strained Jordan's economy and infrastructure, especially its schools, which have had to move to double shifts in order to help accommodate some of the Syrian children. We are working closely with the Jordanian government on solutions to alleviate the strain on the country, both in the short and long term, and in a humane way. During the King's visit, we discussed how to handle ongoing humanitarian challenges for the 22,000 refugees on the Syrian-Jordanian border.

To date, the United States is the largest single donor contributing to the Syria humanitarian response in support of refugees and vulnerable host community members in Jordan. We have provided more than $730 million in humanitarian aid to organizations assisting Syrian refugees in Jordan since the start of the crisis, including more than $62 million announced last week by Secretary Kerry at the Fourth Syrian Donor's Conference in London. These funds also benefit the Jordanian communities that graciously host Syrian refugees. Overall, donors pledged $700 million in additional grants for Jordan for 2016 at the conference last week. In addition, the European Union announced it was working with Jordan on an initiative to facilitate access to the EU market as part of a broader "compact" in which Jordan will provide Syrian refugees with work permits and increased access to education. Implementation of this compact will also help create jobs for Jordanians. We will continue to discuss with the Jordanian government ways in which we can work together to improve the lives of these refugees and address the needs of the communities that graciously host them.

Conclusion

Chairman Ros-Lehtinen, Ranking Member Deutch, our partnership with Jordan remains strong, and our military coordination and assistance has never been closer. From their counter Da'esh activities to Jordan's active participation in a number of peacekeeping operations around the world, Jordan is a strong friend and an essential partner in our pursuit of regional peace and prosperity. Thank you for the opportunity to testify, I look forward to taking your questions.

Ms. Ros-Lehtinen. Thank you so much, Mr. Ambassador. Ms. Alexander.

STATEMENT OF MS. PAIGE ALEXANDER, ASSISTANT ADMINIS-TRATOR, BUREAU FOR THE MIDDLE EAST, U.S. AGENCY FOR INTERNATIONAL DEVELOPMENT

Ms. Alexander. Thank you, Chairman Ros-Lehtinen, Ranking Member Deutch, members of the subcommittee. Thank you for the opportunity to discuss the United States Agency for International Development's assistance to Jordan.

Jordan has one of the largest USAID missions in the world. Our longstanding partnership with the Kingdom dates back nearly six decades.

Over the years this cooperation has improved water systems, trained teachers and enhanced the quality of education. We have also upgraded medical facilities and have increased job opportunities by developing key sectors of the Jordanian economy.

With Congress' generous support in Fiscal Year 2015, $615 million went into the Economic Support Fund programs that directly help the Jordanian people.

Our economic assistance to Jordan is multifaceted, including direct assistance, sovereign loan guarantees and project-based programs.

We are working to help the Government of Jordan deal with the significant development challenges, low economic growth, crowded classrooms and scarce water resources, as you all have discussed.

USAID has reoriented its development assistance to better support the government and the people of Jordan and has addressed the increased needs in the areas and sectors where Syrian refugees have the greatest impact on the Jordanian communities.

We recognize the enormous strain on resources that Jordanians face due to the large population increases from the Syria crisis.

Our programming is designed not only to help host communities meet current needs but also to identify and catalyse innovations that meet Jordan's longer-term development challenges.

My statement for the record includes more details of the USAID priorities and challenges in Jordan. I would like to briefly give you some examples here.

USAID supports the Government of Jordan's reform agenda, focusing on strengthening civil society, rule of law and good governance with partners such as the chairman's mention of IRI.

During my trip to Jordan last year, I met with local officials in communities hosting these large refugee populations. They told me the assistance they received from the American people has been invaluable.

For example, USAID partners with local communities and officials to identify the real stressors and the priorities in community life, and then USAID—with our partners—helps the municipalities implement very practical solutions, things such as paving streets, replacing broken street lights or picking up the trash, which make a major difference in these communities.

USAID's economic development and energy programs in Jordan have evolved over the years from building roads to building a more diverse and globally competitive economy.

One program has awarded nearly 100 grants totalling more than $5 million to small- and medium-sized enterprises.

One of these grants went to the Andalus Dairy Factory run by a local cattle farmer association in northern Jordan. With the help of the project, the factory entered a partnership with Safeway and achieved $140,000 annual increase in revenue and now they are on track to double that increase in the coming year.

We are also the lead donor for education in Jordan where the Syria crisis is having a profound effect on the public schools. To help the Jordanians meet this challenge, USAID has expanded 120 schools, renovated 146 schools and built 25 new schools in areas where there are large population increases from the refugee flows.

We are also fast tracking the expansion of 20 schools in the most needed areas. Just last week, I attended the London conference where Secretary Kerry announced the additional $267 million commitment for education in Jordan.

This will help Jordanian public schools provide quality education for an estimated 230,000 Syrian refugee children and another 500,000 Jordanian students.

I want to share one particularly inspiring story, that of Maha Al Ashqar. She is the principal of the Khawla bint Tha'laba Primary Girls' School.

When a Syrian refugee mother approached the school and wanted to get her child in, she was told that the classes were full. She approached the principal and Ms. Al Ashqar's response was simple—yes, your daughter can come to school, I ask that you bring a chair because we have run out of chairs.

It is by supporting educators and families determined to get ahead that we can make sure more children are not lost to this conflict.

We are also working to ensure that the humanitarian assistance we provide to Syrian refugees has benefits for the local Jordanian economy.

For example, we fund a food voucher debit card for Syrian refugees. I believe the two of you saw this when you were in the camp. I actually brought one because it is nicely branded as well.

And, for example, with these vouchers these cards are used to shop in the local Jordanian supermarkets and stores. They give the users a dignified way to buy food for their families, giving them more choice and nutritional diversity than food handouts would permit.

It has also provided an important economic boost for the host country. It is estimated that the program has injected at least $428 million into the Jordanian economy, providing new jobs and new revenues to food retailers, traders and producers.

Going forward, we need to think about how to preserve the important development gains made through the years of bilateral assistance to Jordan while developing creative solutions that help to meet the complex challenges posed by refugees living in these host communities.

Thank you for the opportunity to appear before you today and I look forward to your questions.

[The prepared statement of Ms. Alexander follows:]

Testimony of
Paige Alexander, Assistant Administrator for the Middle East
United States Agency for International Development
House Foreign Affairs, Subcommittee on Middle East and North Africa
Hearing: "Jordan: A Key U.S. Partner"
February 11, 2016, 2-5 p.m.
2172 Rayburn House Office Building

Introduction

Chairman Ros-Lehtinen, Ranking Member Deutch, distinguished members of the Committee: Thank you for inviting me here today to discuss the work of the U.S. Agency for International Development (USAID) in the Hashemite Kingdom of Jordan. I want to thank you for your unwavering support for USAID's work in Jordan, and in particular for our assistance to the Kingdom as it contends with the spillover effects of the Syria crisis more broadly. I commend you and the Committee for shining a spotlight on the situation, which grows more complex every day.

Jordan—one of our critical allies in the region—hosts one of the largest USAID Missions in the world. Our longstanding partnership with Jordan dates back more than six decades and translates into a high degree of cooperation and coordination with the Jordanian government. Over the years, this cooperation has included support to help augment Jordan's scarce water resources by improving pumping systems and constructing water treatment plants; train teachers and enhance the quality of education; upgrade medical facilities; and increase job opportunities for Jordanians by developing and expanding key sectors of the Jordanian economy. Our work in Jordan helps advance the Agency's overall mission to partner to end extreme poverty and promote resilient, democratic societies while advancing our prosperity and security.

As my colleague PDAS Feierstein noted, we signed a Memorandum of Understanding (MOU) with Jordan last year expressing the intent to provide it with $1 billion per year in security and economic assistance from FY 2015 to FY 2017. With Congress's generous support, in the first year of that MOU, the United States provided over $1.01 billion for Jordan, of which $615 million went into our Economic Support Fund programs. It also supports USAID's country development cooperation strategy to improve prosperity, accountability, and equality for a stable, democratic Jordan.

Jordan faces enormous humanitarian and development challenges stemming from the Syrian crisis. As you know, the record levels of displacement from the five-year Syrian conflict have had a serious impact on neighboring countries, including Jordan. The vast majority of Syrian refugees -- more than 85 percent -- live in host communities, not in camps, straining local infrastructure and essential services. There are more than 635,000 Syrian refugees registered in Jordan, representing a 10 percent increase in population size in just a few years. In some instances, the refugee influx has doubled or tripled the size of Jordanian towns located near the Syria border.

I want to commend the Jordanian people and the Jordanian government for their generous hospitality to these refugees and their strong efforts to address the needs of the refugee population, often in difficult circumstances. USAID has worked diligently to help the Jordanian government and Jordanian people respond to these needs, and we have expanded our development assistance in Jordan to support these host communities.

USAID Assistance to Jordan

Our economic assistance to Jordan is multifaceted, comprising direct assistance, sovereign loan guarantees and project-based assistance.

Since the crisis started, with the generous support of Congress, USAID has provided $1.51 billion in direct assistance to the Government of Jordan (GOJ) to help pay non-military debt and free up resources to attend to the immediate needs of Jordan's population. This assistance is contingent on specific GOJ actions intended to address Jordan's constraints to future growth and supports Jordan's balance of payments position and overall economic stability in light of ongoing regional crises.

Additionally, through three loan guarantees, the U.S. government has guaranteed $3.75 billion in sovereign debt at interest rates that are affordable for the GOJ given the crisis. These guarantees have reduced the interest burden borne by the GOJ, encouraged meaningful economic reforms, and helped build Jordan's ability to access international capital markets. U.S. sovereign loan guarantees help Jordan address the effects of the Syria crisis and incentivize critical reforms that will address the long term needs of the Jordanians.

Prior to the outbreak of the Syrian conflict, Jordan was already dealing with significant development hurdles: low economic growth, low quality of schooling and overcrowded classrooms, inadequate public services, and scarce water resources. The crisis struck the Jordanian economy when it was already suffering from its lowest growth rates in a decade, struggling to keep pace with a burgeoning population growth rate. The flow of Syrian refugees further strained Jordan's already limited water resources. Well into its fifth year, the crisis continues to aggravate these challenges, stretching the social fabric and negatively affecting access to and quality of essential services.

To help respond to these challenges, USAID has also reoriented our development assistance to better support the government and people of Jordan, and address increased needs in areas and sectors where refugees are having the greatest impact on Jordanian communities. We have reviewed our country development cooperation strategy and reformulated our approach to incorporate the longer-term challenges posed by large numbers of refugees into our assistance strategy for Jordan. Our programming is designed not only to help host communities meet current needs, but will also identify and catalyze new and evolving innovations, with the goal of improving the lives of both host communities and refugees living in them.

Governance and Community Engagement

USAID supports the GOJ's reform agenda, focusing on strengthening civil society, rule of law, and good governance. USAID programs aim to expand citizen participation in government, strengthen an independent judiciary, advance human rights, and promote increased transparency and accountability to combat corruption. Programs also focus on building community cohesion and enhanced resilience, particularly in communities affected by the influx of refugees. The refugee influx has contributed to a rise in local tensions, particularly from Jordanians in host communities who are increasing pressure on already strained municipalities to deliver essential services.

During my trip to Jordan last year, I met with Jordanians and Syrians, as well as educators and local officials in communities hosting large refugee populations, who tell me the assistance they receive from the American people helps them do their jobs better. Through our Community Engagement Project, USAID partners with host communities, municipalities and other stakeholders to organize citizen focus groups and surveys that reflect the real stressors and priorities in community life. USAID helps the municipalities find practical solutions to help address these challenges—for example, paving streets, replacing broken street lights or picking up the trash—which helps alleviate these tensions.

USAID also works to advocate and promote gender equality across all programs and sectors. USAID's current strategy is to implement cross-cutting activities that mainstream gender throughout our programs and enhance gender equality and women's empowerment. Programs promote changes in discriminatory social norms and practices, enhance advocacy and policy reforms, expand access to female-centered services, encourage women's participation in the economy, and empower women to play an active role as citizens and policymakers.

Economic Growth

Jordan continues to struggle with low economic growth rates and insufficient job creation, challenges that have been heightened by the refugee influx. In 2013, the unemployment rate for women was about twice that of men, and for youth between the ages of 15-24 it stood above 30 percent. USAID's economic development and energy programs in Jordan have evolved over the years from building roads to building a more diverse and globally competitive economy. During the past decade, USAID has partnered with the GOJ to implement fiscal reforms, promote trade, investment and job creation, enhance competitiveness in the private sector, increase energy efficiency and improve workforce readiness. USAID's work helped facilitate Jordan's accession to the World Trade Organization and its use of the U.S.-Jordan Free Trade Agreement (FTA). Trade between Jordan the U.S. before the FTA was $400 million; in 2014, it was $3.5 billion.

One program, the USAID Local Enterprise Support Project, is encouraging long-term economic growth and development of underserved Jordanian communities by supporting the competitiveness of micro and small enterprises (MSEs) that are often at the heart of individual, family and community livelihoods within vulnerable populations. The project helps to empower local communities to design and implement local economic development initiatives. To date, the project has awarded more than 82 grants, totaling more than $5 million, to new and existing MSEs, Micro-Finance Institutions and Businesses Service Providers that will generate increased revenue, create new jobs, and enhance the businesses environment. One of these grants went to Andalus Dairy Factory, run by a local cattle farmers' association in northern Jordan, which with the help of the project entered a partnership with Safeway and achieved a $140,000 annual increase in revenue. They are on track to double that revenue in the coming year.

Additionally, USAID is helping create a more competitive, demand-driven workforce that will lead to increased private sector employment, especially for Jordan's women, youth and those living at or below the poverty line. Working in six governorates, USAID engages with the private sector to develop new and enhance existing vocational and technical education programs in targeted industries. Whether it is improving the rules on workplace safety or strengthening certification and accreditation standards, USAID is working to ensure that the labor force has the skills and capabilities necessary to meet the private sector's labor demands into the foreseeable future. Through this $40 million investment, USAID estimates that it will provide improved employment opportunities for 25,000 Jordanians over five years.

We are also seeking to understand better the impact of Syrian refugees on the Jordanian economy. USAID is involved with two important studies to help illuminate where and how to harness the valuable human capital that resides in the Syrian refugee population. We are working with the Jordanian Ministry of Labor to undertake a labor market study that will provide insights into which sectors of the Jordanian economy employ third country nationals—not Jordanians— that might be able to substitute Syrian labor. We are also working on a household level survey that will look at the impact of Syrians as investors, consumers and employees and that will verify information that we have about the skill set Syrians can potentially bring to the workforce. Ideally, we are looking to find "win-wins" that help catalyze economic growth, creating jobs and growth opportunities for both Jordanians and Syrians living in Jordan.

Health

The demand on the public health sector continues to grow, affecting access and quality of services for all residents of Jordan. The capacity of Jordan's public health sector to deliver adequate services has been stretched at all levels, a situation that has been exacerbated by conflict-related injuries and disabilities and the re-emergence of some communicable diseases. USAID is investing in the construction and renovation of maternal and pediatric health facilities across Jordan, increasing the GOJ's ability to provide essential health services to Jordanians as well as Syrian refugees. Maternal, newborn and child healthcare activities focus on improving key aspects of in-hospital obstetrical and neonatal care and scaling-up advanced interventions, reducing preventable maternal and child deaths. USAID's efforts have helped reduce infant mortality from 30 deaths per 1,000 live births in 1997 to 17 deaths per 1,000 live births in 2012. USAID also focuses on improving the quality of healthcare systems through enhancing service delivery, workforce development, knowledge and information systems management and infrastructure improvements, which will strengthen the resiliency of the Jordanian health system.

Education

USAID education and youth programs seek to strengthen the public education system, improve the quality of education and learning outcomes and improve access to education and learning environments.

We are the lead donor for education in Jordan, where the crisis is having a profound impact on the education sector, particularly public schools. By the end of 2015, 145,000 Syrian refugee children were enrolled in Jordanian public schools, straining the capacity of these schools. The GOJ has reintroduced double-shift schedules in 98 of the most overcrowded public schools to accommodate this demand and has provided pre-fabricated classrooms in other cases. To help the situation, USAID is expanding 120 schools, renovating 146 schools and building 25 new schools in areas with large numbers of Syrian refugees. We are also fast-tracking the expansion of 20 schools in overcrowded areas. And just last week, I attended the London Conference where Secretary Kerry announced a $267 million commitment for education in Jordan, which will help Jordanian public schools provide a quality education for the estimated 230,000 Syrian refugee children and 500,000 Jordanian students.

We are also helping Jordan provide learning environments where all children can thrive. We are supporting the Ministry of Education with a $48 million early grade reading and math development project for all primary school students in Jordan to help maintain the quality of education as the number of students in Jordanian schools rises. The reading and math project includes training for 13,500 teachers. We are also training 4,000 teachers in Jordan so that they can counsel Syrian refugee children who, at best, may struggle to fit in, and at worst may grapple with the trauma of violence and abuse. USAID is also supporting remedial programs so that refugee students can make up years of lost schooling.

Our education team recently shared one particularly inspiring story: that of Maha Al Ashqar, the principal of the Khawla Bint Tha'laba Primary Girls School. When a Syrian refugee mother showed up at the school gates last year, desperate to enroll her daughter, she was told the school year had started and classes were full. The determined mother asked to speak to the principal. Ms. Al Ashqar's response was simple: "Yes your daughter can come. I just ask that you bring a chair because we do not have any left." The school has also recruited mothers as teaching aides to keep up with the larger class sizes. By supporting educators and families determined to get ahead, we can make sure more children are not lost to this conflict.

Water

Jordan is one of the driest countries on Earth, and demand for water exceeds Jordan's renewable freshwater sources. Water networks are outdated and in serious need of rehabilitation. USAID is improving water resource management through demand management, improved pricing, integrated water resources management, and improving water and wastewater infrastructure helping to address the additional strain on water resources caused the increase in population. USAID's efforts have helped increase potable water supplies in Jordan by 10 percent over the past decade. For example, USAID constructed rainwater harvesting cisterns for households and community centers in Irbid and Mafraq governorates—which host large concentrations of refugees—helping these communities save much needed water. USAID's work to rehabilitate and renovate the Zabdah reservoir, Jaber treatment plant and pump station, and Tabaqet Fahel well saved around 600 cubic meters of water per hour, enough to serve 180,000 persons per day. We are also supporting the construction of a new pipeline, pump station and waste water treatment plant that will increase water supply and waste treatment for 1.7 million in northern Jordan.

Humanitarian Assistance

About half of the $5.1 billion of life-saving humanitarian assistance the United States has provided to date in the Syrian crisis goes to Syrian refugees living in neighboring countries. This assistance seeks to fill critical immediate needs such as food, clean water, sanitation and shelter.

Food assistance comprises a large component of our aid, and in Jordan we fund an innovative program, run by the World Food Program (WFP), which provides food voucher debit cards to Syrian refugees. These debit-card vouchers are used to shop in local Jordanian supermarkets and stores, giving the users a dignified way to buy food for their families, with greater nutritional diversity than they would receive from food distribution, while also providing an important economic boost to the host country. It is estimated that the WFP program has injected at least $428 million into the Jordanian economy, providing new jobs and new revenue to food retailers, traders and producers. The electronic voucher program is just one example of an innovative idea to make sure that our assistance benefits not only refugees, but the communities that host them.

We are working closely with our colleagues in the State Department to make sure we have a joint long-term vision for our humanitarian and development programs.

The Way Forward

While USAID has re-oriented its bilateral assistance to better address the impact of Syrian refugees in Jordan, we will need to continue to adapt and innovate given the long-term effects. As the Syrian conflict extends into its sixth year, it is clear that humanitarian assistance alone is not sufficient to address the crisis. Often unable to work legally and without other means of support, the vulnerability of refugees is deepening. They are increasingly forced to rely on negative coping strategies: taking on debt or living in overcrowded housing. Child labor, begging, and early marriage are all on the rise.

With our colleagues in the State Department and other international donors, and especially with our Jordanian partners, we are striving to develop innovative solutions. We are particularly focused on the critical areas of education and livelihoods, which face challenges keenly felt by both refugees and host communities.

Going forward, we need to think about how to preserve the important development gains made through years of bilateral assistance to Jordan, while developing creative solutions that help meet the complex challenges posed by the rapid expansion of host communities to temporarily accommodate refugees. Ideally, we need to find ways to catalyze the potential gains refugee populations can contribute to host communities, tapping this important flow of human capital and finding ways to transform the refugee challenge into opportunity. We need to ensure that both host communities and refugees are on a sustainable, positive development trajectory. USAID remains committed to supporting the long term development of Jordan while also supporting the Syrian refugees in Jordan and the communities so generously hosting them.

Thank you for the opportunity to appear before you today. I look forward to your questions.

Ms. Ros-Lehtinen. Thank you so much, Ms. Alexander.

Ms. Sumar.

STATEMENT OF MS. FATEMA Z. SUMAR, REGIONAL DEPUTY VICE PRESIDENT, EUROPE, ASIA, THE PACIFIC AND LATIN AMERICA, DEPARTMENT OF COMPACT OPERATIONS, MILLENNIUM CHALLENGE CORPORATION

Ms. Sumar. Well, thank you so much and good afternoon.

Thank you, Chairman Ros-Lehtinen, Ranking Member Deutch and members of the subcommittee for the opportunity to discuss the Millennium Challenge Corporation's work with our partners in Jordan to fight poverty.

I request that my full written testimony be submitted for the record.

Ms. Ros-Lehtinen. Without objection.

Ms. Sumar. MCC forms partnerships with some of the world's poorest countries, but only those committed to good governance, economic freedom and investment in their citizens.

MCC provides these select countries, like Jordan, with grants to fund country-led projects and reforms designed to reduce poverty by promoting sustainable economic growth.

MCC's Board of Directors selected Jordan as eligible for a threshold program in 2005. The threshold program supported Jordan's efforts to strengthen local government by increasing transparency and accountability.

The program also sought to enhance the efficiency and effectiveness of their customs administration as a way to encourage trade. Our $275 million compact with Jordan began implementation in December 2011 and will end in December of this year.

Because Jordan is one of the most water-scarce countries in the world, our compact focuses on increasing the supply of water available to households and businesses and improving the efficiency of water delivery, wastewater collection and wastewater treatment.

Affordable access to clean water is critical not just for businesses and agricultural producers but for all Jordanians. The scarcity and expense of water constrains the country's economic potential.

Though our partnership began before the crisis in Syria erupted, Jordan's generous response to that crisis has only compounded the strain on the country's water supply, making MCC's work there even more critical.

The compact includes three closely-related projects to address the needs of the goverment's entire water system. First, as you saw during your visit there, the biggest investment of the compact is the expansion of the As-Samra Wastewater Treatment Plant, originally built with support from USAID.

It is the primary facility for treating wastewater from Jordan's Amman and Zarqa governorates where much of the country's population lives.

The expansion increased the plant's capacity by more than one-third, while more than doubling its capacity to handle certain chemicals and other materials.

It now treats 70 percent of the country's wastewater. One of the most interesting aspects of this project is its innovative financing.

MCC's grant is paying for the expansion in partnership with a private sector operator. This public-private partnership allowed MCC's investment of $93 million to mobilize an additional $110 million from the private sector.

Through this financing method, the private sector not only provides over 50 percent of the cost of construction, it also ensures that the facility is operated and maintained at world class standards for 25 years.

Second, the wastewater network project will modernize and upgrade the outdated sewer system in Zarqa. This project has already replaced or rehabilitated trunk sewer lines and expanded the system by laying over a 139 miles of sewer pipe.

And third, our water network restructuring project—before this project, if you can imagine, as much as 50 percent of water that entered the system was lost both through leaks in the network and weak management—an unsustainably high loss rate, given Jordan's scarce water resources.

This third project has repaired reservoirs and pumping stations, and already replaced more than 70 percent of the targeted 495 miles of urban drinking water pipelines.

What is perhaps most notable about this program and about all of MCC's compacts with our partner countries is that it is the Jordanians who determined which problem we should address and how we should tackle it.

Following the end of our engagement with our partner countries, we perform impact evaluations where possible to see how successful our projects were in reducing poverty.

In Jordan, we are implementing an innovative impact evaluation of the benefits of our projects to Jordanian households and farmers.

This impact evaluation will be one of the first of its kind to measure the economic benefits of improved water infrastructure. The success of this evaluation and of our overall compact is a product of the close relationship between MCC and the Government of Jordan.

The Government of Jordan has been an excellent partner in the development and implementation of the compact.

Thank you again for the invitation to testify, and I look forward to answering any questions.

[The prepared statement of Ms. Sumar follows:]

TESTIMONY

House Foreign Affairs Committee
Subcommittee on the Middle East and North Africa
"Jordan: A Key U.S. Partner"

Statement by
Fatema Z. Sumar
Deputy Vice President for Europe, Asia, the Pacific, and Latin America
Department of Compact Operations
Millennium Challenge Corporation

February 11, 2016

Thank you Chairman Ros-Lehtinen, Ranking Member Deutch, and members of the Subcommittee on the Middle East and North Africa for the opportunity to discuss the Millennium Challenge Corporation's (MCC) work with our partners in Jordan to fight poverty.

MCC forms partnerships with some of the world's poorest countries—but only those committed to good governance, economic freedom, and investments in their citizens. MCC provides these select countries, like Jordan, with grants to fund country-led projects and reforms designed to reduce poverty by promoting sustainable economic growth. There are two kinds of MCC grants: compacts and threshold programs. Jordan has had one of each.

Our engagement with Jordan, like our work with many of our partner countries, began with one of our smaller threshold programs. Threshold programs seek to provide promising countries with a potential gateway to compact eligibility. A successful threshold program seeks to achieve three objectives: (1) boost the "MCC Effect" by incentivizing partner countries' greater commitment to investing in people, economic freedom, and ruling justly; (2) invest in policy and institutional reforms critical to growth and good governance; and (3) assess the opportunity for a compact partnership.

MCC's Board of Directors selected Jordan as eligible for a threshold program in 2005. Jordan's program, which USAID implemented under our old threshold program framework, began in 2006 and was completed in 2009. The program supported Jordan's efforts to strengthen municipal government by increasing transparency and accountability in local government, deepening public interaction with elected officials and improving the quality of planning and economic development at the local level. The program also sought to enhance the efficiency and effectiveness of customs administration as a way to encourage trade.

The threshold program helped reduce customs clearance and processing times, sometimes by as much as 80%. The program also supported efforts to increase women and youth participation in local elections, including launching a "Get out the Vote" campaign in districts across the country. The Women's Knowledge Network, supported by the program, created a forum for discussion and support among newly elected women in public service on municipal councils. The program further helped to improve local governance capacity by assisting municipal staff in creating three-year development plans and increasing coordination with the private sector.

With good performance on the threshold program, and passage of MCC's scorecard in 2006 and 2007, MCC's Board of Directors selected Jordan as eligible for a compact in November 2006. Compacts are our larger, five-year assistance programs which combine major infrastructure investments with complementary policy reforms.

Our $275.1 million Compact with Jordan began implementation in December 2011, and will conclude in December 2016. Because Jordan is one of the most water scarce countries in the world, our Compact focused on increasing the supply of water available to households and businesses and improving the efficiency of water delivery, wastewater collection, and wastewater treatment. Affordable access to clean water is critical—not just for businesses and agricultural producers, but for all Jordanians. The scarcity and expense of water in Jordan constrains the country's economic potential. Though our partnership began before the crisis in Syria erupted, Jordan's generous response to that crisis has only compounded the strain on the country's water supply, making our work there even more critical.

MCC's Compact is designed to increase the supply of water through improvements in water delivery, wastewater collection and wastewater treatment. Once completed, the Compact is expected to benefit approximately 3 million people. The Compact includes three closely-related projects to address the needs of the governorate's entire water system:

1. **As-Samra Wastewater Treatment Plant Expansion project.** The biggest investment of the Compact is in the expansion of the As-Samra Wastewater Treatment plant, originally built with support from USAID. It is the primary facility for treating wastewater from Jordan's Amman and Zarqa Governorates—where much of the country's population lives. The expansion increased the plant's capacity by more than one-third, while more than doubling its capacity to handle certain chemicals and other materials. It now treats 70% of the country's wastewater.

   By treating much of the country's wastewater to an extremely high quality, the plant also provides more than 10% of Jordan's total irrigation water resources for use in the Jordan Valley—freeing up fresh water for municipal use. As a byproduct of wastewater treatment, the plant also provides bio-solids for potential re-use in fertilizer and fuel, and produces nearly 13 megawatts of energy, or 80% of its own energy needs, from biogas and hydropower.

   One of the most interesting aspects of this project is its innovative financing. MCC's grant is paying for the expansion in partnership with a private sector operator, which contributed to the cost of construction and agreed to operate and maintain the plant for a period of 25 years. This Public Private Partnership allowed MCC's investment of $93 million to mobilize an additional $110 million from the private sector. Through this financing method, the private sector not only provides over 50% of the cost of construction, but it assures the government that the facility is operated and maintained at world class standards for 25 years. The plant is the first large-scale public-private partnership project to be directly supported with MCC funds, and—because of its success to date in pairing limited public resources with investment from private companies— serves as a model for how MCC plans to engage the private sector to accelerate economic growth in its partner countries. The project has won international awards, including the "Water and Energy Exchange International Award for Innovative Financing," and the "Best Water Project Award" by World Finance Magazine.

2. **The Wastewater Network Project.** This project will modernize and upgrade the outdated sewer system in Zarqa Governorate, the country's second largest city and home to a significant population of ethnic minorities and Palestinian and Iraqi refugees. The old system regularly overflowed into the streets and served less than three quarters of the population when it worked. This project has already replaced or rehabilitated trunk sewer

lines and expanded the system by laying over 139 miles (225km) of sewer pipe in two chronically underserved neighborhoods. This extension will raise coverage rates in the Governorate to 85%. Because of cost-savings, this project was able to well exceed its original targets, and is now on track to complete a total of 186 miles (300km). The new connections and the rehabilitated system will dramatically reduce sewage overflows into city streets, and supply the treatment plant with additional wastewater to meet its newly expanded capacity. Additionally, the Government of Jordan contributed $20 million to expand wastewater pumping stations, complementing MCC's investments in this sector.

3. **Water Network restructuring**. The Water Network project aims to reduce water losses in the governorate's drinking water system. Before rehabilitation, as much as 57% of the water that entered the system was lost, both through leaks in the network and weak management—an unsustainably high loss rate, given Jordan's scarce water resources. The project has repaired reservoirs and pumping stations, and already replaced more than 70% of the targeted 495 miles (800km) of urban drinking water pipelines. This project is also replacing household connections and water meters through the "Water Smart Homes" activity aimed at improving the efficiency of water use and reducing water expenditures among the poorest households. Over 1,500 such home repairs have been completed to date. The project is also providing certified plumbing training for women, and providing targeted grants to assist in efficient water management.

The combined Compact investments in water, wastewater, and water treatment, will directly benefit over three million citizens of Zarqa and Amman.

What's perhaps most notable about this program—and about all of MCC's compacts with our partner countries—is that it's the Jordanians who determined which problem we should address, and how we should tackle it. We worked together to conduct analyses and identify priorities, but our Jordanian partners really did "own" the process. This country ownership continues into the project implementation phase, and contributes to the long-term sustainability of our investment—it is the Jordanians who are implementing these projects, with appropriate MCC oversight. This is important to MCC because we know that if our partners really care about how we jointly spend our dollars, they will do a better job of taking care of that investment over the long term.

MCC's partnership with Jordan has been one of our most successful, including MCC's first large-scale Public-Private Partnership in infrastructure, and on-time, under-budget construction of some truly transformational water infrastructure. Should you travel to Jordan, I encourage you to take the time to see our projects for yourselves.

That said, MCC's engagement with our partner countries is time-limited, and after December 2016, our Compact with Jordan will be closed and we will no longer be working with the Jordanians, though we have worked with them to ensure that our investments will be sustained and maintained after we leave. Additionally, during MCC's engagement with Jordan, the country's average gross national income level has increased to the point that it has "graduated" from the pool of countries that our statute permits us to partner with. These firm time and income limits are parts of our model, which aims to break the binding constraints to economic growth and give countries the tools they need to lift themselves out of poverty.

Following the end of our engagement with our partner countries, we perform impact evaluations where possible to see how successful our projects were at reducing poverty. These impact evaluations are in addition to the simpler performance evaluations that we perform as we implement our compacts. Both impact and performance evaluations tell us how effective we were and help us design better compacts in the future.

In Jordan, we are implementing an innovative impact evaluation of the benefits of our projects to Jordanian households and farmers. Simply put, our evaluation will measure the cost savings each household will get from the additional hours of running water (before our Compact, households averaged only 36 hours of running water every week during the summer). We will also capture the benefits to farmers of an increased supply of treated wastewater for agriculture. This impact evaluation will be one of the first of its kind to measure the economic benefits of improved water infrastructure.

The success of this evaluation, and of our Compact, is a product of the close relationship between MCC and the Government of Jordan, who has been an excellent partner in the development and implementation of this Compact.

Thank you again for the invitation to testify on MCC's work with Jordan. I am happy to take any questions you may have on MCC, our model, or our work in Jordan.

———

Ms. ROS-LEHTINEN. Thank you so much for excellent presentations. I will begin the question and answer period.

One of Jordan's critical needs is energy, although not as burdensome now since, thankfully, oil prices have taken dive. But Jordan has almost no domestic production to talk about, importing around 97 percent of its energy needs.

The agreement to import natural gas from Israel could be a game changer, not just for Jordan and Israel but for the entire region.

Ambassador Feierstein, would you talk about the significant foreign policy benefits for all parties involved with this agreement? What has the U.S. been doing to promote these exports, given that there have been some challenges faced on both sides?

Ambassador FEIERSTEIN. Absolutely, Congresswoman Ros-Lehtinen.

The United States has been strongly supporting the efforts of the two parties with Noble Energy, an American energy provider, to reach agreement to draw natural gas from the Leviathan Field as well as the Tamar Field in Israel and those talks are going forward with a great deal of encouragement from the United States.

Our acting assistant secretary for energy, Amos Hochstein, has been very much involved in promoting the efforts and discussing this and we are optimistic that these—that these contracts will be completed and that the gas will be provided to Jordan.

As you said quite correctly, it's going to be a significant bonus for Jordan, a reliable sustainable source of energy for them to fuel their economic growth and development going forward.

Ms. ROS-LEHTINEN. Thank you. And, Ambassador, water is also a critical need. In the Fiscal Year 2016 omnibus bill, Congress appropriated $100 million in Economic Support Funds to be set aside to Jordan for supporting its Red to Dead Canal Project pending completion of the relevant studies and assessment.

How are—where are we on those assessments? What obstacles are needed to be overcome in over to get this project up and running?

Ambassador FEIERSTEIN. Thank you, and absolutely we appreciated the congressional decision to provide $100 million for the Red to Dead effort.

We are engaged very closely with the Government of Jordan as well as with the Israelis and the Palestinians, pushing that forward.

As you noted, and Ms. Alexander may be able to comment as well, we are engaged in the effort to complete the environmental impact studies and the other work that is necessary.

But we also believe that we are moving closer, perhaps in another month or two, to having a meeting that will bring all of the parties together to continue the design work and to further the implementation of that project.

Ms. ROS-LEHTINEN. Thank you, sir.

And, Ms. Alexander, you noted that Jordan hosts one of the largest USAID missions of the world and we also noted not just the willingness of the government to work with our mission but that the Jordanian people very much welcome a lot of the work that we do there.

The Kingdom represents a relatively open space and a difficult region for civil society and the sort of work that USAID is looking to expand on in areas that it is hoping to strengthen.

Does Jordan's willingness to work on these issues suggest an opportunity for increased support for democratic institutions?

What would that look like and are we focusing too much of our assistance on meeting the needs of the Syrian refugees and not enough on Jordan's actual development needs?

And I encourage USAID to explore new entities, a new partnership with groups who have a proven track record of local democratic governance in Jordan.

What type of local government assistance gives us the ability to strengthen the stability of a country like Jordan, given the immense pressure that it is under?

Ms. ALEXANDER. Thank you.

I agree that the global economic crisis has really undermined all the previous gains that the Jordanian Government had had—reduced exports, remittances, reduced tourism revenue, as referenced before, and foreign direct investments.

So the loss of this and then the trading partners of Egypt, Syria and Iraq that had been such a valued part of the economy and the economic development for Jordan has really set them back.

However, having such an excellent partnership with the Jordanian Government, we have continued to work very closely on the Jordan response plan and reoriented our assistance to make sure that we are addressing their needs as well as the stressors on the sectors, whether it is education, health, or water.

So I think the partnership is valuable. I would not say that there is a lack of understanding between the need between the Syrian refugees and the host communities.

I think that we are working very hard to make sure that we are addressing the Jordanian Government's concern about that.

Ms. ROS-LEHTINEN. And finally, as I mentioned earlier, Congressman Deutch and I visited that wastewater project during our last visit to Jordan together and it was remarkable how much progress had been made on such an important issue for Jordan—water—and I think that—I know that Jordan's MCC contract is completed at the end of this year—the compact focused on three major water projects.

But Ms. Sumar, with Jordan being such an important player for the region and its stability vital to ensuring that the entire region doesn't descend into something much worse, do you think that Jordan would be a good contender for a second MCC contract—compact and, if so, what areas would be best to focus on for future projects?

Ms. SUMAR. Well, thank you, Madam Chairman, for the question and thank you for taking the time to visit the plant during your visit to Jordan.

As you noted, we have had terrific success in this compact because of the strong partnership we have with the Government of Jordan and our implementing partner, the Millennium Challenge Account in Jordan.

According to our statute from Congress—our legislation, we are both time-bound in the way we operate but we are also bound by income levels. MCC only works in countries with both low income and lower middle income status as defined by the World Bank.

Currently, starting in Fiscal Year 2012, Jordan graduated from lower middle income status and is currently an upper middle income country.

There are ongoing negotiations and conversations, I understand, between the Government of Jordan and the World Bank on its population numbers, given the flows from the refugee crisis, which could change some of those calculations, given its GNI per capita.

We look forward to hearing the decision from the World Bank, which is where we get our data from. But currently Jordan would not be a contender for a second compact because it has graduated to upper middle income status and that is a consideration that we have to take seriously in our legislation.

Ms. ROS-LEHTINEN. Thank you so much.

And I would like to yield now to my great colleague, Congressman Deutch.

Mr. DEUTCH. Thank you, Madam Chairman.

Ms. Alexander, outside of the refugee-specific initiatives, what other successes can you point to in supporting job creation initiatives in Jordan?

Ms. ALEXANDER. Thank you.

Our economic development assistance has worked on everything from fiscal reforms at the ministries to make sure we have long-term sustainability and better procedures in place.

We have also worked in the health care sector and I would say that building maternal and child health care—child facilities and pediatric facilities—we have modernized the health workforce and we have established a health quality assurance mechanism.

The financial sustainability of almost all of the issues including water is a major one, as referenced earlier, with 90 percent of the water imported—gas and energy, sorry, imported. That has become a major issue for us.

In the water sector we are looking at nonrevenue water loss and working directly with the ministries to make sure that they are tightening up their systems.

So I would say it is on a fiscal side with the ministries as well on the local government side with making sure that civil society is listened to in a lot of these communities that are suffering from stress.

Mr. DEUTCH. Great. Thanks.

Ambassador Feierstein, King Abdullah makes very strong pronouncements in the international community that Arab states must lead the fight against ISIS.

Can you just share your insight as to whether the Jordanian public is still supportive of the country's involvement and leadership role in the campaign against ISIS?

Ambassador FEIERSTEIN. Thank you, Congressman Deutch.

I believe that our assessment is that there is still a high level of support within the Jordanian community for the effort to combat violent extremism.

The King and the Government of Jordan have done a good job of trying to explain to the Jordanian people what the challenges are, what the threat is to Jordanian security and stability.

He has engaged broadly with not only the political leaders but also with religious leaders, motivating and energizing imams to speak out in the mosques against the threat of violent extremism.

And in this context, I think that the Jordanians have really been leaders not only in terms of how they have approached the challenge and the issues within Jordan but also in trying to assist and to build a broader Sunni Arab coalition that speaks out very strongly against this threat.

Mr. DEUTCH. How helpful do you think the King can be with respect to halting Russian aggression against the moderate opposition in Syria? Is there a role for the King there?

Ambassador FEIERSTEIN. Well, this is an important issue and, of course, as you know, the King did try to engage the Russians in an effort to prevent the expansion of the conflict toward the Jordanian borders in southern Syria.

Our understanding, based on our discussions with him, is that he has been disappointed, of course, in the lack of Russian responsiveness, although when he discussed this directly with President Putin he was under the impression that the Russians would be cooperative with this effort.

To be entirely honest, we were skeptical of the effort and we remain skeptical. But the King believes that this is an important element and that he needs to be able to speak to the Russians and try to get the Syrian Government to go along with this.

So he is going to continue to try. But I think that at this point he is a little bit more skeptical and wary about how the Russians might respond.

Mr. DEUTCH. Great.

And then, finally, just turning away from Jordan just for a second since you are here, I understand there is legislation in the Senate, the Justice Against Sponsors of Terrorism Act, that passed out of the Senate Judiciary Committee recently, and as a member of both Foreign Affairs and Judiciary Committees here in the House, I have an interest in that.

Since you are here, I thought I would ask whether the department has a position on this bill.

Ambassador FEIERSTEIN. Thank you very much for that question, Congressman Deutch, and we do.

We understand and sympathize with the motivation behind the JASTA legislation. The proposed remedy, however, would enact broad changes in longstanding international law regarding sovereign immunity that, if applied globally, could have serious implications for U.S. interests.

Before proceeding with the legislation, we believe there needs to be more careful consideration of the potential unintended consequences of its enactment and we would welcome opportunities to engage with the Congress in that discussion.

Mr. DEUTCH. Thank you, Mr. Ambassador.

Thanks to all of our witnesses for being here today.

Ms. ROS-LEHTINEN. Thank you, Mr. Deutch.

Mr. Rohrabacher.

Mr. ROHRABACHER. First and foremost, I would like to thank you, Madam Chairman, for your leadership over the years.

I have been serving in Congress with you for 28 years and you have been a dynamo on those issues that are vital to our national security and to human rights as well. So thank you for bring this up today.

Because today you have focused our attention on a country that is indispensable to the cause of peace in the Middle East. Without Jordan, we all lose.

Everybody loses if Jordan succumbs to radicalization, and I would say that we need to pay this kind of attention all the time toward this.

Let me ask a little bit about the—I learned a long time ago. My parents came from dirt-poor farms in North Dakota and that was long before they had any of the oil or anything up there. And I was taught that people can't be prosperous—ordinary people can't live a prosperous and decent life without enough energy but also enough water.

And you were just going through in the testimony the water projects and how much money has been put into that. Is there still a water shortage in Jordan after the investment that we have made?

Ms. ALEXANDER. I will say yes. It has been the third most water-scarce country in the world and so this is why a lot of our assistance at USAID has focused on issues such as nonrevenue water loss and, specifically, reforming and restructuring how to make this system more efficient.

I will turn it to my colleague to talk about the MCC work.

Mr. ROHRABACHER. Right.

Ms. SUMAR. Certainly, Congressman, it is—not only is it one of the most water scarce countries in the world, it is a country that is strained under burgeoning population flows.

And so the investments that MCC has been making over the past 5 years are intended to not only take a look at the current needs of the Jordanian people in the cities but also take a long-term view of the kind of economic growth that is——

Mr. ROHRABACHER. Is it based on reclamation? Is that your—the system that you have been providing support for in Jordan?

Ms. SUMAR. It is based on three different principals. One is that we need to add different parts of wastewater treatment so that you don't have sewage flowing over into your major cities and streets.

In order to do that, we built this signature project, which is the As-Samra Wastewater Treatment Plant. Connected to that are wastewater pipes that would be needed to actually pipe out the sewage from the cities into the treatment plants. So we have built hundreds of kilometers of those pipes.

But the third part of that and particularly most important for people's everyday lives is to make sure they also have the drinking water that they need and the drinking supplies.

So the third component is building the water pipes for drinking water. As a result of that entire holistic intervention, what we are seeing is not just piping the wastewater out, treating and cleaning it but pumping that water in a clean way back into the irrigation system of Jordan.

So one of the biggest results we have seen is we have freed up to 10 percent of water to use for irrigation in the Jordan River Valley. That is fresh water that we are now putting back into the system and it is increasing its availability for farmers and beneficiaries alike.

Mr. ROHRABACHER. Well, just to let you know, I come from Orange County, California, and in Orange County we are on a desert and we have a water system now—reclamation system in which we reuse our water nine times before it is let out into the ocean.

And I would hope that that type of gray—with the use of technology we can help solve that problem and we should certainly be sharing that technology with the people of Jordan.

And second of all, about the Red Sea to Dead Sea project, is that going to be a reality? This is something that is going on that provides both energy and water, does it not?

Ms. ALEXANDER. As my colleague had previously mentioned, we are working to understand a long-term economic viability of the project and to ensure that we have plans in place to mitigate any environmental impacts of the project.

We have worked very closely with our colleagues at State and consulting with the Jordanians and the Israeli Government and we do think there is a meeting coming up where the next phase of this will be discussed.

Mr. ROHRABACHER. I am concerned, frankly, and Madam Chairman, we see this here in the United States as well. There are, you know, people who believe the environment and keeping it a clean environment is their number-one priority and sometimes they are a little bit too, how do you say, unrealistic about the cost of having a 95-percent situation rather than a 100-percent situation.

And the Red Sea to Dead Sea project has been going on for a long time and offers such a great potential for benefit for economic, and economic benefit means how good—how well people are living—ordinary people—and I would hope that people who are taking the extreme positions on the environment are not undermining the well being of women and children who are trying to live their lives today, which I think would be greatly benefited by that project.

With that said, we ought to do everything we can and thank you for leading the effort to do something good for a good friend of the United States.

Thank you, Madam Chairman.

Ms. ROS-LEHTINEN. Thank you so much, Mr. Rohrabacher.

And thank you to our panelists for excellent testimony. Thank you to the Ambassador for joining us, and with that the subcommittee is adjourned because we will have votes in about 5 minutes.

Thank you so much.

[Whereupon, at 3:04 p.m., the committee was adjourned.

APPENDIX

SUBCOMMITTEE HEARING NOTICE
COMMITTEE ON FOREIGN AFFAIRS
U.S. HOUSE OF REPRESENTATIVES
WASHINGTON, DC 20515-6128

Subcommittee on the Middle East and North Africa
Ileana Ros-Lehtinen (R-FL), Chairman

February 4, 2016

TO: MEMBERS OF THE COMMITTEE ON FOREIGN AFFAIRS

You are respectfully requested to attend an OPEN hearing of the Committee on Foreign Affairs, to be held by the Subcommittee on the Middle East and North Africa in Room 2172 of the Rayburn House Office Building (and available live on the Committee website at http://www.ForeignAffairs.house.gov):

DATE   Thursday, February 11, 2016

TIME: 2:00 p.m.

SUBJECT: Jordan: A Key U.S. Partner

WITNESSES: The Honorable Gerald M. Feierstein
                   Principal Deputy Assistant Secretary
                   Bureau of Near Eastern Affairs
                   U.S. Department of State

                   Ms. Paige Alexander
                   Assistant Administrator
                   Bureau for the Middle East
                   U.S. Agency for International Development

                   Ms. Fatema Z. Sumar
                   Regional Deputy Vice President
                   Europe, Asia, the Pacific and Latin America
                   Department of Compact Operations
                   Millennium Challenge Corporation

By Direction of the Chairman

The Committee on Foreign Affairs seeks to make its facilities accessible to persons with disabilities. If you are in need of special accommodations, please call 202/225-5021 at least four business days in advance of the event, whenever practicable. Questions with regard to special accommodations in general (including availability of Committee materials in alternative formats and assistive listening devices) may be directed to the Committee.

COMMITTEE ON FOREIGN AFFAIRS

MINUTES OF SUBCOMMITTEE ON _____ *Middle East and North Africa* _____ HEARING

Day____*Thursday*____Date_____*2/11/16*_____Room_____*2172*_____

Starting Time ____*2:00 p.m.*____ Ending Time ____*3:04 p.m.*____

Recesses __*0*__ (____to ____) (____to ____) (____to ____) (____to ____) (____to ____) (____to ____)

Presiding Member(s)

Chairman Ros-Lehtinen

Check all of the following that apply:

Open Session ☑   Electronically Recorded (taped) ☑
Executive (closed) Session ☑   Stenographic Record ☑
Televised ☑

TITLE OF HEARING:

Jordan: A Key U.S. Partner

SUBCOMMITTEE MEMBERS PRESENT:

Chairman Ros-Lehtinen, Reps. Chabot, DeSantis, Meadows, Clawson, Zeldin, Deutch, Connolly, Cicilline, Grayson, Meng, Frankel and Boyle.

NON-SUBCOMMITTEE MEMBERS PRESENT: *(Mark with an * if they are not members of full committee.)*

Rep. Rohrabacher

HEARING WITNESSES: Same as meeting notice attached? Yes ☑ No ☐
(If "no", please list below and include title, agency, department, or organization.)

STATEMENTS FOR THE RECORD: *(List any statements submitted for the record.)*

TIME SCHEDULED TO RECONVENE _____
or
TIME ADJOURNED ____*3:04 p.m.*____

_____
Subcommittee Staff Director

**Questions for the Record Submitted to
Principal Deputy Assistant Secretary Gerald Feierstein by
Representative Ileana Ros-Lehtinen
House Committee on Foreign Affairs
February 11, 2016**

Question:

Can you provide insights into how the government plans to spend the additional development assistance it has committed (beyond education funding)?

Answer:

On February 4 at the London Conference on Syria, Secretary Kerry announced that the United States will provide nearly $601 million in additional life-saving humanitarian assistance for those affected by the war in Syria. This funding brings U.S. humanitarian assistance in response to this conflict to more than $5.1 billion since the start of the crisis. Secretary Kerry also announced more than $290 million in U.S. development assistance for education to Jordan and Lebanon. This assistance will continue and extend our support to the Jordanian and Lebanese ministries of education in their goal of increasing access to high-quality education and supporting learning for all students, including Syrian refugees. Our education assistance will reach approximately 195,000 Syrian refugees in Jordan, and 62,000 in Lebanon.

The development assistance announced at the London Conference reflects the United States' commitment to education. The U.S. will continue to build upon these investments with future resources, pending availability of funding. The State Department and USAID are committed to working with Congress to provide continued funding to address these critical needs.

Question:

How is the administration planning to implement the new Section 7063 – "Countries impacted by significant refugee populations or internally displaced person"[1] which provides greater funding flexibility to address the needs of host communities as well as refugees?

Answer:

The refugee influx due to the war in Syria has stretched already limited resources and imposed severe stress on Jordan's economy, municipalities, fiscal balance, and public services. The GOJ recently unveiled the Jordan Compact: a new holistic approach to deal with the Syrian refugee crisis including commitments by both Jordan and the international community. The United States is fully supportive of the Jordan Compact, and will refocus its bilateral assistance program in Jordan to address the Compact's key goals, such as facilitating investment, spurring private sector job growth for Jordanians and Syrians, bolstering the implementation of the Jordan Response Plan, and supporting Jordan's macroeconomic stability.

Through USAID programming, the United States is examining new approaches to help Jordan meet the needs of Syrian refugees and of the Jordanian population, scaling up existing services, matching Jordanians and Syrians with jobs, investing in health and education, and attracting and facilitating investments, so that refugees and Jordanians alike can share in progress and move forward together. Modified and new programming will bolster communities supporting Syrian refugees with a focus on self-reliance, access to enhanced public services, spurring job growth, and fostering economic inclusion.

---

[1] [1]COUNTRIES IMPACTED BY SIGNIFICANT REFUGEE POPULATIONS OR INTERNALLY DISPLACED PERSONS SEC. 7063. Funds appropriated by this Act under the headings "Development Assistance" and "Economic Support Fund" shall be made available for programs in countries affected by significant populations of internally displaced persons or refugees to—
(1) expand and improve host government social services and basic infrastructure to accommodate the needs of such populations and persons;
(2) alleviate the social and economic strains placed on host communities;
(3) improve coordination of such assistance in a more effective and sustainable manner; and
(4) leverage increased assistance from donors other than the United States Government for central governments and local communities in such countries.
Sec. 7063. Countries Impacted by Significant Refugee Populations or Internally Displaced Persons (New) The agreement includes language in section 7063 modified from that proposed in section 7081 of the Senate bill, except the Secretary of State is directed to submit the report required in section 7081 (b) in the manner described in such section. In lieu of the information required in section 7081(b)(3), the Secretary of the Treasury is directed to submit a report to the Committees on Appropriations, not later than 90 days after enactment of this Act, on the implications for country access to World Bank and other concessional lending and grants if the World Bank were to modify its per capita income categories to reflect the impact of significant refugee populations and internally displaced persons on host communities.
Not later than 90 days after enactment of this Act, the CEO of the MCC is directed to submit a report to the Committees on Appropriations on the number of middle income countries that would become eligible for MCC compacts, and any other implications for MCC operations and programs of such updated World Bank per capita income categories.

Question:

Can you each speak to how your individual agency (State, USAID, MCC) is taking this new provision into account as you plan your FY16 programming?

Answer:

In FY 2016, the Department and USAID will continue to coordinate with the Jordanian government's Jordan Response Plan (JRP) to address refugee needs. More specifically, with U.S. government funding we will increase provision of safe and protective learning spaces and facilities for Jordanian and Syrian children; build the capacity of government to provide high quality, integrated health services that can respond to the growing needs of changing demographics; enhance long-term job growth through demand-based vocational training and job matching; support the establishment and growth of micro, small, and medium enterprises; improve municipal service delivery in host communities; expand transport services and systems to accommodate increased population in the northern governorates; and improve the management and conservation of water resources.

Question:

Can you please elaborate on how democracy assistance to Jordan in the future will be implemented to effectively strengthen local governance?

Answer:

USAID/Jordan will strengthen the ability of elected officials at the sub-national level (Governorate Councils, mayors, municipal and local councils) to serve their constituents. Development assistance will establish and streamline processes and systems for efficient human resource management – particularly hiring processes – and public financial management, including revenue generation. Assistance will also enable municipalities to improve the provision of core services, such as solid waste management. USAID assistance will enable sub-national-level officials to increase their outreach to citizens through the use of town hall meetings, hearings and technology; and USAID will support citizens to more effectively engage with their representatives. USAID will also help municipalities, as the level of government closest to citizens, to increase social cohesion and improve community resilience as a result of the Syrian refugee crisis through community events, specific efforts for inclusion of marginalized groups, and other activities.

Question:

What is the justification for the mechanism selected to provide future assistance to strengthen local governance in Jordan?

Answer:

The impact of the Syrian crisis on Jordan, particularly the influx of Syrian refugees that has dramatically increased the population of some municipalities, has created potentially de-stabilizing conditions that require USAID's technical direction and day-to-day oversight of implementation. USAID's planned assistance is multi-faceted. Its complexity during this critical period in Jordan as the country grapples with regional turmoil, particularly the crisis in the north, necessitates USAID's involvement in the awardee's programmatic approach in order to ensure performance and results in an ever-evolving refugee crisis. In addition, due to the rapidly changing environments in the municipalities, USAID will provide technical direction over specific deliverables, such as those falling under the service delivery and the social cohesion components of the activity. Finally, assistance will support governance under the newly enacted decentralization framework, which links municipalities to the soon to be created Governorate Councils. Given the uncertainties of the implementation of the decentralization framework, USAID's close technical direction and oversight will help ensure that assistance appropriately responds to the evolving context. In conclusion, USAID/Jordan has reviewed the changing nature of the Syrian crises in Jordan, and has determined that the nature of the intended relationship has changed in which the Mission now has a more direct need for engagement on the envisioned services in accordance with federal regulations and agency policies related to selecting the appropriate implementing mechanism.

Questions for the Record
for USAID Assistant Administrator Paige Alexander
from Chairman Ros-Lehtinen
Jordan: A Key Partner
2/11/16

1. The London Conference on Syria took place on February 4th. The U.S. State Department announced over $925 million in additional assistance to the Syria Crisis. Secretary Kerry pledged more than $600 million in life-saving humanitarian assistance and $325 million in development assistance – including $290 million for education to Jordan and Lebanon.

    Can you provide insights into how the government plans to spend the additional development assistance it has committed (beyond education funding)?

    The $290 million in development assistance announced at the London Conference pertained to the U.S. commitment for education. Nothing beyond education was pledged in London. This assistance will continue and extend our support to the Jordanian and Lebanese ministries of education in their goal to increase access to high-quality education and to support learning for all students, including Syrian refugees. This $290 million did not include the additional FY 2017 budget request.

    The U.S. will continue to build upon these investments with future resources, pending availability of funding. The State Department and USAID are committed to working with Congress to provide continued funding to address these critical needs.

2. The Government of Jordan has taken on an enormous role by officially hosting at least 635,000 registered Syrian refugees, the actual overall number is likely twice as high (1.3 million) – this amounts to roughly 10% of the Jordanian population. We applaud the commitment that the Jordanian government has made to support the needs of these refugees.

How is the administration planning to implement the new Section 7063 – "Countries impacted by significant refugee populations or internally displaced person"[1] which provides greater funding flexibility to address the needs of host communities as well as refugees?

The refugee influx due to the war in Syria has stretched already limited resources and imposed severe stress on Jordan's economy, host communities, fiscal balance, and public services. The Government of Jordan announced the Jordan Compact at the February 4 London conference on Syria: an agreement to provide work permits to Syrians in exchange for relaxed rules of origin with the European Union and a concessional finance facility with the World Bank for refugee-related projects.. The U.S. government is supportive of the Jordan Compact, and USAID will focus relevant parts of its assistance program (both existing and planned) in Jordan to address the Compact's key goals, such as facilitating investment, spurring private sector job growth for Jordanians and Syrian refugees, bolstering the implementation of the Jordan Response Plan, and supporting Jordan's macroeconomic stability.

USAID is examining new approaches to help Jordan meet the needs of Syrian refugees and of the Jordanian population, such as: scaling up existing services; matching Jordanians and Syrian refugees with jobs, investing in health and education, and; attracting and facilitating investments so that refugees and Jordanians alike can share in progress and move forward together. Modified and new programming will bolster communities supporting Syrian refugees with a focus on self-reliance, access to enhanced public services, spurring job growth, and fostering economic inclusion.

Can you each speak to how your individual agency (State, USAID, MCC) is taking this new provision into account as you plan your FY16 programming?

In FY 2016, USAID/Jordan plans to continue coordination through the Jordan Response Plan (JRP) to address refugee needs. More specifically, USAID will focus efforts to: increase provision of safe learning spaces and facilities for Jordanian and Syrian refugee children; build the capacity of government to provide high quality, integrated health services that can respond to the growing needs of changing demographics; enhance long-term job growth through demand-based vocational training and job matching; support the establishment and growth of micro, small, and medium enterprises; improve municipal service delivery in host communities; expand transport services and systems to accommodate increased population in the northern governorates, and; improve the management and conservation of water resources.

3. As your testimony has demonstrated, USAID's programming to strengthen local governance in Jordan has resulted in impressive outcomes. I understand that future local governance programming is scheduled to be procured utilizing the Indefinite Quantity Contract mechanism, a departure from the Cooperative Agreement mechanism that has yielded such strong results to date.

Can you please elaborate on how democracy assistance to Jordan in the future will be implemented to effectively strengthen local governance?

USAID/Jordan will strengthen the ability of elected officials at the sub-national level (Governorate Councils, mayors, municipal and local councils) to serve their constituents. Development assistance will establish and streamline processes and systems for efficient human resource management – particularly hiring processes – and public financial management, including revenue generation. Assistance will also enable municipalities to improve the provision of core services, such as solid waste management. USAID assistance will enable sub-national level officials to increase their outreach to citizens through the use of town hall meetings, hearings and technology, and USAID will support citizens to more effectively engage with their representatives. USAID will also help municipalities, as the level of government closest to citizens, to increase social cohesion and improve community resilience through community events, specific efforts for inclusion of marginalized groups, and other activities.

What is the justification for the mechanism selected to provide future assistance to strengthen local governance in Jordan?"

The impact of the Syrian crisis on Jordan, particularly the influx of Syrian refugees that dramatically increased the population of some municipalities, created potentially de-stabilizing conditions that require USAID's technical direction and day-to-day oversight of implementation. The Indefinite Quantity Contract mechanism enables such strengthened direction and oversight. USAID's planned assistance is multi-faceted. Its complexity during this critical period in Jordan as the country grapples with regional turmoil, particularly the crisis in the north, necessitates USAID's involvement in the awardee's programmatic approach to ensure performance and results in an ever-evolving refugee crisis. In addition, due to the rapidly changing environment in the municipalities, USAID will provide technical direction for specific deliverables, such as those falling under the service delivery and the social cohesion components of the activity. Finally, assistance will support governance under the newly enacted decentralization framework, which links municipalities to the soon-to-be-created Governorate Councils. Given the uncertainties of the implementation of the decentralization framework, USAID's close technical direction and oversight, as required under contractual agreements, will ensure that assistance appropriately responds to the evolving context. USAID/Jordan reviewed the program in light of the changing nature of the Syrian crisis in Jordan and determined that the Mission should have more direct engagement with the envisioned services in accordance with federal regulations and agency policies related to selecting the appropriate implementing mechanism.